Royale Equestrian Centre

Royale Equestrian Centre

Siena's Stories 3

ISBN: 978-1-990818-26-4

© Siena 2025

MotherButterfly
Books

www.motherbutterfly.com

This book is dedicated to the master comic book artist and art instructor, Geof Isherwood.

A true mentor of young artists and a friend.

The first day of Spring. I am so excited!

Today, I get my first riding lesson at Royale Equestrian Centre in my home city of Ottawa, Ontario, Canada.

While my daddy drives,
I sing songs in my car seat.

Royale Equestrian Centre is surrounded by a wooden fence. There is one entrance with a beautiful iron gate decorated with horses.

Inside the fence is a farmhouse.

A 100 year old barn.

A large outdoor riding area.

Indoor riding arenas so we can ride in any weather.

Emily Bertrand founded
Royale Equestrian Centre.
She will be my instructor today.

Emily takes me to the tack room in the old barn to get me fitted for my helmet. My friends Alexi and Noemi are also here for a lesson.

My horse Riding equipment:

helmet →

Riding
gloves

paddock
boots

What I need to wear
to stay safe while
riding.

half
chaps

Body Brush

Mane and Tail Brush

Face Brush

Curry Comb

Shedding blade

Hoof Pick / Brush

I collect brushes for my grooming kit.

Today, I am going to ride a pony named Tea Biscuit.

With a little help, I get Tea Biscuit's bridle and saddle.

An important first step is to brush Tea Biscuit.

Dandy Brush

Hoof Pick

Curry Comb

I use a curry comb, hoof pick and a dandy brush.

I use the hoof brush to clean out Tea Biscuit's hooves. Emily explains that a part of the hoof is called the "frog."

Siena humorously imagines a frog jumping from Tea Biscuit's hoof.

I put on Tea Biscuit's saddle pad and saddle.

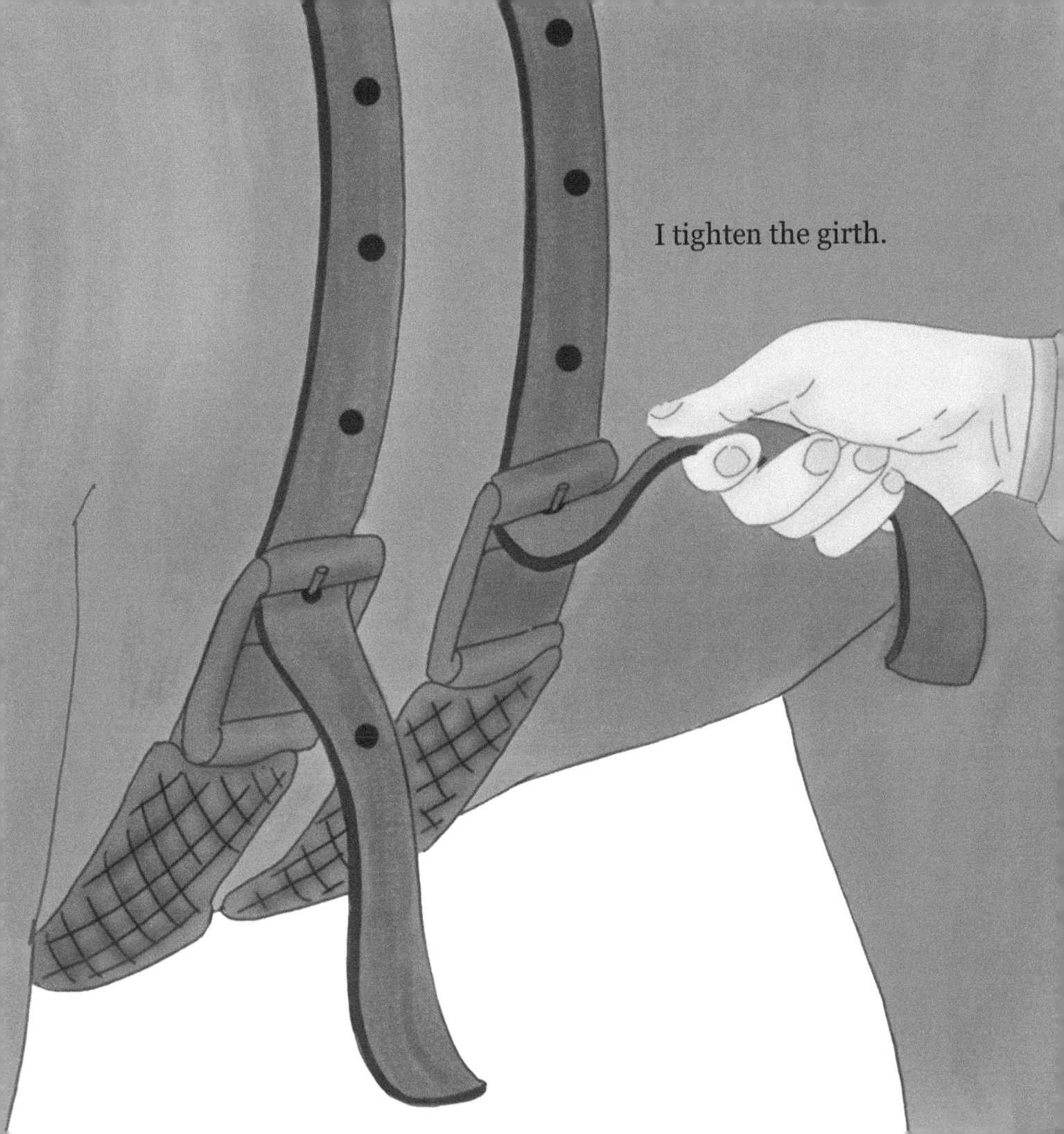

I tighten the girth.

The bridle goes on carefully
and I secure it.

Ready to ride!

We lead Tea Biscuit to an indoor arena.
My friend Ian has just finished his lesson.
He is riding Indy.

Ready to mount Tea Biscuit.

Practice basic walking. Emily holds a lead rope for safety.

I make sure I have the proper grip.

Proper riding posture:

Eyes up.
Straight line ear-shoulder-hip.
Heels down.
Hands on reins.

Hands on hips to test balance.

Airplane!

Emily claps and states that I did a great job.

After dismounting,
I give Tea Biscuit a kiss.

On the ride home, I shared my experiences with my daddy.

About Emily Bertrand

As Founder & CEO at Royale Equestrian Centre. Emily is fueled by her love and passion for horses and sharing this passion with others.

Royale Equestrian Centre located in Ottawa Ontario was started by Emily and her mother Dawn Patterson on July 1st, 2007. The farm was named after Emily's horse at the time, Royale. A blood bay Irish thoroughbred.

Emily started riding at the age of four and was instantly hooked. She has a unique perspective drawing on years of diverse experience from a variety of disciplines and successful roles in the equine industry. From riding or competing in eventing, show jumping, hunters, western, breeding, driving draft horses, starting, and retraining, coaching, even calf sorting.

Emily is very passionate about horse care, horsemanship, and the training and development of horses and riders. With the help of an outstanding team, she has developed an incredible framework and program that specializes in teaching people of all ages how to ride and care for horses. The cornerstone of the program is in offering a welcoming, positive, and friendly environment that educates and inspires.

Offering unique never seen before programs and opportunities. Royale Equestrian Centre is a leader in providing quality riding lessons, camps, and programs such as Equine First Aid, and helping students to become certified coaches.

In 2020 Emily embarked on building a second facility Royale Ranch along side her cousin Cody Czeitler and family friends, the Calder Family.

About Anna Davydova

Anna lives in Canada, Ottawa. She is a passionate artist and children's book illustrator who loves creating cute and heartwarming images. As a nature lover, Anna finds inspiration in the beauty of the world around her. She usually uses Photoshop, Illustrator, and Procreate.

Anna likes to imitate traditional materials like pencils and colours digitally, but she also paints traditionally using watercolours. Additionally, Anna is a caring mom who is inspired by her three beautiful children.

Get FREE books!

Go to :
motherbutterfly.com